Sam, Kim and Ravi did not want to

"Let's have a sleep-out," said Sam.
"Yes! We can have a sleep-out in my garden," said Ravi.

They put their sleeping bags in the garden.
"Sleep well," said Ravi's mum.

It was getting dark. They all got into their sleeping bags.

"Ouch!" said Kim. "Who bashed my chin?"
"Not me," said Ravi.
"Not me," said Sam.

"Ouch!" said Ravi. "Who bashed **my** chin?"
"Not me," said Kim.
"Not me," said Sam.

"I don't like this sleep-out," said Kim.
"Don't be such a baby," said Sam.

"I don't like this sleep-out," said Ravi.
"Don't be such a baby!" said Sam.

"Ouch! Ouch! Ouch!" said Sam. "Who bashed **my** chin?"
"Not me," said Ravi.
"Not me," said Kim.

"Get the torch, Sam!" said Kim.
"Get the torch, Sam!" said Ravi.

Sam got the torch.
"Look!" he said. "What's that up there?"

"It's got wings," said Kim, "and it's got ears."

"It's got big wings," said Ravi, "and it's got big ears!"
"What has got big wings and big ears?" said Sam.

"Bats!" said Kim.
"Bats!" said Ravi.
"Bats!" said Sam. "Wow!"

"Was it a bat that bashed my chin?" said Kim.
"No," said Sam. "Look!"